DBT WORKBOOK FOR CLINICIANS

The DBT Clinician's Guide to Holistic Healing Integrating Mind, Body, and Emotion

This workbook, tailored specifically for modern therapists, extends beyond the confines of traditional methodologies.

Lucia Alarm

ISBN- 978-1-917186-87-2

Gaius Quill Publishing

DBT WORKBOOK FOR CLINICIANS

Venturing beyond traditional DBT, this workbook introduces an interdisciplinary approach. Clinicians are armed with exercises blending mindfulness, somatic techniques, and cognitive strategies to offer a more holistic healing journey. The emphasis is on addressing both mental and physiological aspects of distress, ensuring patients attain a deeper, lasting relief.

Table of Contents

Author's Note

In the journey of creating "The DBT Clinician's Guide to Holistic Healing: Integrating Mind, Body, and Emotion," my intent has always been to bridge the established principles of Dialectical Behavior Therapy (DBT) with the broader, interrelated spectrums of mind, body, and emotion. It is a culmination of years of research, clinical experience, and personal introspection.

I've always believed that the essence of therapeutic intervention is not just to alleviate distress but to guide individuals toward holistic well-being. In this endeavor, it becomes imperative for clinicians to be equipped with a diverse toolkit that addresses the interconnectedness of the human psyche and physiology. This book is my humble attempt to present such an interdisciplinary approach.

While every effort has been made to ensure the accuracy and reliability of the information presented, therapeutic strategies should always be tailored to individual needs and circumstances. The case studies, while based on real experiences, have been modified to maintain confidentiality. Feedback, critiques, and shared experiences from fellow clinicians will be invaluable in refining and evolving the presented approach.

Thank you for embarking on this journey with me. I hope it proves to be as transformative for you as it has been for me.

Disclaimer:

All names and identifying details in the case studies presented in this book are entirely fictional. Any resemblance to actual persons, living or dead, is unintentional and purely coincidental. These names have been created solely for the purpose of illustrating the concepts and scenarios within the book, and they do not reflect or represent any real individuals.

Introduction

Brief overview of DBT and its core components.

Certainly! Dialectical Behavior Therapy (DBT) is a cognitive-behavioral treatment developed by Dr. Marsha Linehan in the late 1980s. It was originally designed to treat individuals with borderline personality disorder (BPD) and those exhibiting chronic suicidal behavior. However, its applications have since expanded to treat a variety of other conditions, including substance use disorders, eating disorders, and PTSD. DBT blends cognitive-behavioral techniques with Eastern mindfulness practices.

DBT's Core Components:

1. **Mindfulness:** This is the foundational component of DBT. Mindfulness involves being fully present in the moment and accepting it without judgment. It helps individuals distinguish between thoughts, feelings, and sensations and fosters an acceptance of reality as it is.

2. **Distress Tolerance:** This module teaches individuals how to tolerate pain in difficult situations, not change it. It emphasizes coping techniques that can help during crises, such as distraction, self-soothing, and considering the pros and cons of a situation.

3. **Emotion Regulation:** Here, individuals learn to recognize and label their emotions, understand the triggers that lead to intense emotions, and develop

coping strategies. This component teaches skills like reducing vulnerability to emotional triggers, increasing positive emotional events, and applying distress tolerance techniques.

4. **Interpersonal Effectiveness:** This involves techniques to ask for what one needs, how to assertively say 'no,' and how to cope with interpersonal conflict. The skills taught in this module are designed to foster effective communication, strengthen relationships, maintain self-respect, and achieve interpersonal objectives.

5. **Walking the Middle Path (added later for adolescents and their families):** This module focuses on balancing acceptance and change, recognizing both sides of a situation, and finding a compromise. It's especially useful when dealing with polarized thinking patterns.

Modes of Treatment in DBT:

1. **Individual Therapy:** One-on-one sessions between the patient and therapist, addressing the patient's most pressing concerns and reinforcing the application of DBT skills.

2. **Group Skills Training:** Group sessions where individuals learn and practice the DBT skills, led by a trained therapist. Each of the core components mentioned above is taught in these sessions.

3. **Phone Coaching:** Patients can call their therapists between sessions for guidance on applying skills to real-life situations.

4. **Consultation Team for Therapists:** A support group for DBT therapists, ensuring that they also receive guidance, support, and motivation to provide the best possible care.

DBT stands out because of its emphasis on dialectical thinking, which involves holding two seemingly opposite perspectives at once, such as accepting oneself as is while also acknowledging the need for change. This balanced perspective promotes both change and acceptance, which are crucial for therapeutic progress.

Introduction to the Holistic Approach in DBT

Dialectical Behavior Therapy (DBT) inherently emphasizes the synthesis of opposites—most notably, the balance between acceptance and change. Building upon this foundation, a holistic approach to DBT aims to consider the whole individual, integrating mind, body, and spirit in the therapeutic process. This means addressing not just cognitive and behavioral patterns, but also the interconnectedness of physiological, emotional, social, and spiritual aspects of well-being.

Why Holistic?

The term 'holistic' comes from the Greek word 'holos,' meaning 'whole.' Instead of focusing solely on symptoms or behaviors, a holistic approach seeks to understand and address the entirety of a person's experience. This is particularly fitting for DBT, which already emphasizes the interplay between acceptance and change.

Components of a Holistic Approach in DBT:

1. **Mind:** Traditional DBT already places emphasis on cognitive processes. In a holistic model, the depth of understanding one's thought patterns, beliefs, and inner narratives is further explored, often incorporating techniques from other therapeutic modalities.

2. **Body:** Recognizing that the body stores trauma, emotions, and memories, a holistic DBT approach may integrate somatic therapies. This could include methods like mindful movement, breathwork, or even addressing dietary and sleep patterns—anything that acknowledges the role of physical well-being in emotional health.

3. **Emotion:** While DBT inherently addresses emotional regulation, a holistic approach further deepens this exploration, often delving into the origins of emotions, the connection between emotions and bodily sensations, and the link between emotions and spiritual experiences.

4. **Spirit:** This isn't necessarily religious (though it can be, depending on the individual). It refers to one's connection to purpose, meaning, and a sense of something greater. A holistic approach in DBT may integrate practices like meditation, exploration of personal values, or even nature therapy.

Benefits of a Holistic Approach:

- **Comprehensive Care:** By addressing all facets of an individual, therapists can facilitate deeper healing and more sustained well-being.
- **Enhanced Self-awareness:** Clients can develop a deeper understanding of their triggers, responses, and needs by examining themselves from multiple angles.
- **Versatility:** Therapists have a broader toolkit, drawing from a range of techniques and strategies to best meet the client's needs.

Incorporating Holistic Techniques:

Therapists may weave in elements like guided visualizations, grounding exercises, journaling prompts, or even recommendations related to physical activity and nutrition. They might explore spiritual beliefs that influence one's thought patterns or incorporate practices that connect one with nature, community, or a higher purpose.

In summary, while traditional DBT offers a potent framework for managing intense emotions and fostering behavioral change, integrating a holistic approach ensures that all layers of an individual's experience are acknowledged and nurtured. By addressing mind, body, emotion, and spirit, DBT can be enhanced, offering clients a more comprehensive and deeply resonant healing journey.

Case Study 1

Case Study: Elena's Journey to Wholeness

Background:
Elena, a 29-year-old graphic designer, sought therapy after experiencing a series of panic attacks at work. A successful professional, she seemed to have everything in order—yet beneath the surface, she grappled with chronic feelings of emptiness, intense mood swings, and difficulty in her relationships.

Initial Assessment:
In her initial DBT sessions, Elena exhibited classic signs of emotional dysregulation common in borderline personality disorder. She had a history of tumultuous relationships, often feeling misunderstood and abandoned, leading her to adopt a coping mechanism of pushing people away preemptively. She also described a profound disconnect between her mind and body, often feeling "numb" or "out of place."

The Holistic Approach:

While traditional DBT techniques were introduced to help Elena manage her acute emotional crises, her therapist also recognized the need for a more holistic approach. Here's how it was implemented:

1. **Mind:** Cognitive exercises helped Elena recognize and challenge her core beliefs, especially those revolving around self-worth and fear of abandonment.

2. **Body:** Elena had a history of trauma, and she often felt disconnected from her body. Through somatic exercises, she was reintroduced to bodily sensations in a safe environment. Simple activities, such as mindful breathing or grounding exercises, were incorporated. Over time, she was introduced to yoga, which became a transformative practice for her.

3. **Emotion:** Elena was encouraged to maintain an emotion diary, where she not only recorded what she felt but also identified triggers and bodily sensations associated with these emotions. It helped her foresee and understand emotional surges before they became overwhelming.

4. **Spirit:** Elena, having grown up in a nature-loving family, reconnected with this aspect by taking regular nature walks, practicing outdoor meditation, and even indulging in weekend hikes.

This rekindled her connection to something bigger than herself and became a source of grounding.

Outcome:
After several months of holistic DBT, Elena began to notice changes. Her panic attacks became less frequent, and when they did occur, she had tools to manage them effectively. She started to build deeper connections, rekindling old friendships and even embarking on a healthy romantic relationship.

But perhaps the most profound change was her renewed sense of self. Elena described feeling "whole" for the first time in years. While challenges remained, she now faced them with resilience, self-awareness, and a support system fortified by her holistic DBT experience.

Conclusion:
Elena's story underscores the power of a holistic approach in DBT. By addressing the interconnectedness of mind, body, emotion, and spirit, individuals can embark on a more comprehensive and deeply resonant healing journey.

Reflection Space

1. After reading Elena's story, what resonated with you the most about her experience with holistic DBT?

....

....

....

....

2. Based on your current understanding, how do you perceive the importance of integrating mind, body, emotion, and spirit in the therapeutic process?

....

....

....

....

3. Think about the clients you currently work with or have worked with in the past. Can you identify any who might benefit from a more holistic approach? Why?

....

....

....

....

4. What are your initial expectations or hopes for integrating a holistic approach in your practice?

....

....

....

....

5. Do you have any concerns or reservations about implementing a holistic approach in DBT? If so, what are they?

....

....

....

....

Feel free to revisit this space as you delve deeper into the book, noting how your perspectives evolve over time.

Chapter 1: Foundations of Holistic Healing in DBT

Traditional principles of DBT.

Dialectical Behavior Therapy (DBT), developed by Dr. Marsha Linehan, was initially formulated to treat individuals with borderline personality disorder, especially those displaying suicidal behaviors. However, over time, its scope has expanded to address other conditions and behavioral issues.

DBT integrates principles from cognitive-behavioral therapy with elements from Zen and contemplative practices, focusing on the synthesis of acceptance and change. This "dialectical" approach gives DBT its distinctive characteristic.

Traditional Principles of DBT:

1. **Dialectical Worldview:** This foundational principle emphasizes that everything is interconnected, that change is constant, and that opposing truths can coexist. The central dialectic in DBT is between acceptance and change. This worldview encourages patients and therapists to work towards synthesizing these opposite perspectives to achieve balance and avoid "black and white" thinking.

2. **Behavioral Target Hierarchy:** In standard DBT, there is a clear hierarchy of behaviors to be addressed:

- Life-threatening behaviors (e.g., suicidal or self-harm behaviors)
- Therapy-interfering behaviors (e.g., coming late to sessions, not doing homework)
- Quality of life-interfering behaviors (e.g., substance abuse, relationship issues)
- Skills acquisition, where patients learn the DBT skills
- Addressing traumas and PTSD (once the previous targets are addressed)

3. **Validation:** This principle involves acknowledging and affirming the patient's feelings, thoughts, and behaviors. Validation helps in reducing patients' suffering and can facilitate the acceptance of painful realities.
4. **Commitment to Treatment:** Both therapists and patients make a clear commitment to the therapy process and the treatment goals. This mutual commitment lays the foundation for a strong therapeutic alliance.
5. **Skills Training:** DBT is well-known for its skills modules, which provide practical tools and strategies for patients to manage their emotions, relationships, and stress. These skills are typically taught in group settings and include:

- Mindfulness
- Distress Tolerance
- Emotion Regulation
- Interpersonal Effectiveness

6. **Contingency Management:** This principle is grounded in behaviorism. It involves reinforcing desired behaviors and applying consequences for undesired behaviors. The aim is to promote functional behaviors and reduce maladaptive ones.

7. **Cognitive Interventions:** These strategies are used to identify and challenge unhelpful beliefs, attitudes, and thoughts that contribute to emotional distress and problematic behaviors.

8. **Exposure:** This involves confronting and experiencing distressing emotions, thoughts, or situations in a controlled and therapeutic manner to reduce avoidance and promote emotional processing.

9. **Stylistic Strategies:** These refer to the unique ways in which DBT therapists interact with patients, such as using irreverence (a playful, non-orthodox approach to challenge maladaptive behaviors or beliefs) or "extending the metaphor" to explain concepts.

10. **Consultation Teams for Therapists:** DBT therapists typically participate in consultation teams to support, guide, and motivate each other. This ensures therapists adhere to the DBT model and provides them with necessary support.

In essence, DBT's traditional principles emphasize a balanced, validating, and skills-based approach to therapy. The dialectical worldview underscores all interventions, ensuring that both acceptance and change are integral to the therapeutic journey.

The Mind-Body-Emotion Connection

The concept of the mind-body-emotion connection posits that our thoughts, feelings, and physical body are intricately linked. Instead of treating each component in isolation, it acknowledges their mutual influence on overall well-being. This interconnectedness means that a change in one area can lead to changes in the others.

The Dynamics of the Connection:

1. **Mind-Body Link:** Thoughts and beliefs can elicit physiological responses. For instance, chronic stress or anxiety (a mental state) can lead to physical symptoms such as high blood pressure, weakened immune function, or digestive issues. Conversely, physical ailments or fatigue can influence our mental state, making us feel down or less optimistic.

2. **Emotion-Body Link:** Emotions often manifest as physical sensations in the body. When you're nervous, you might feel "butterflies" in your stomach, or when you're embarrassed, you might blush. Long-term emotional distress can exacerbate chronic illnesses or cause symptoms like tension headaches or stomach problems.

3. **Mind-Emotion Link:** Thoughts directly influence our emotions. Negative self-talk or rumination can foster feelings of sadness, anxiety, or anger. On the other hand, practicing positive affirmations or gratitude can uplift our mood.

Examples of the Mind-Body-Emotion Connection:

1. **Test Anxiety:** A student named Rahul constantly fears failing his exams (mind). As the exam date approaches, he begins to experience stomach cramps and headaches (body). These physical symptoms make him even more anxious, leading to feelings of dread and panic (emotion).

2. **Public Speaking:** Maria has to give a presentation at work. Just the thought of speaking in front of her colleagues makes her nervous (mind). On the day of the presentation, she notices her heart rate increasing and her palms sweating (body). These physiological changes heighten her feelings of anxiety and insecurity (emotion).

3. **Breakup Grief:** After a breakup, Jake constantly thinks about the loss and what went wrong (mind). He struggles with sleep disturbances and a loss of appetite (body). This physical distress compounds his feelings of sadness and loneliness (emotion).

4. **Physical Rehabilitation:** Lucy was in an accident that left her with a leg injury. During her rehab, she's often frustrated by her body's limitations and fears she won't recover fully (mind). This worry translates into muscle tension and pain during her therapy sessions (body). This physical pain then deepens her feelings of hopelessness and depression (emotion).

5. **Meditative Calm:** On the positive side, consider Anika, who has started practicing daily meditation. The practice helps her cultivate positive, grounding thoughts (mind). Over time, she notices reduced muscle tension, better sleep, and improved digestion (body). These physical benefits bolster her overall sense of peace and emotional balance (emotion).

Understanding this intricate interplay provides a foundation for holistic healing and therapy approaches. By addressing issues in one domain, positive changes can ripple through the others, fostering overall well-being and resilience.

Case Study 2

Case Study: Layla's Dual Journey

Background:

Layla, a 32-year-old teacher, had struggled with intense mood swings, impulsivity, and a pattern of unstable relationships for several years. A traumatic childhood with instances of neglect left her often feeling empty and with a pervasive fear of abandonment.

Journey with Traditional DBT:

Layla's initial therapy was rooted in traditional DBT after she was diagnosed with borderline personality disorder.

1. **Skills Training:** Layla attended weekly group sessions, learning the core DBT modules of Mindfulness, Distress Tolerance, Emotion Regulation, and Interpersonal Effectiveness.

2. **Individual Therapy:** Through one-on-one sessions, she learned to challenge black-and-white thinking, and her therapist consistently validated her emotions, helping her to build trust.

3. **Phone Coaching:** During times of acute distress, Layla could call her therapist for guidance on using DBT skills in challenging situations.

4. **Outcomes:** Layla made progress, particularly in handling acute emotional distress and reducing instances of self-harming behaviors. However, she still felt a persistent disconnect with her body and

struggled with feelings of emptiness and chronic tension.

Shift to a Holistic Approach:
Given the plateau in Layla's progress, her therapist suggested integrating a holistic approach alongside traditional DBT.

1. **Mind:** While continuing cognitive interventions from DBT, Layla also began practices like guided imagery and visualization, connecting deeper with her inner self and challenging core negative beliefs.

2. **Body:** Somatic therapies were introduced. Layla took up tai chi and grounding exercises that helped her reconnect with her body. Regular body scans in therapy sessions enabled her to identify and release pockets of tension, addressing her chronic discomfort.

3. **Emotion:** Layla engaged in art therapy, allowing her to express complex emotions non-verbally. Journaling further helped her map out emotional patterns and triggers, deepening her understanding of her emotional landscape.

4. **Spirit:** Layla began practicing nature mindfulness, spending time outdoors and feeling connected to the world around her. This significantly alleviated feelings of emptiness, replacing them with a sense of belonging and purpose.

Outcomes:

With the holistic approach, Layla experienced a deeper sense of healing. She reported not just a reduction in acute distress (as with traditional DBT) but also a profound feeling of being "in sync" with herself. Her relationships improved, with friends noting that she seemed "more present" and "at peace." Layla's persistent body discomfort diminished, and she felt more complete and connected.

Conclusion:

While traditional DBT provided Layla with essential tools to manage her borderline personality disorder symptoms, the integration of a holistic approach addressed underlying issues, offering a more profound and sustainable healing journey. This case underscores the potential benefits of weaving holistic interventions with traditional therapeutic models.

Reflection Space

1. Reflecting on your current practices, which therapeutic models do you primarily use? Why have you chosen these models, and in what ways have they been effective for your clients?

....

....

....

....

2. Are there clients you've worked with where traditional approaches didn't yield the desired outcomes? What were the challenges faced?

....
....

....
....

3. How familiar are you with integrating holistic healing modalities into traditional therapy approaches? Have you tried any, and if so, what has been your experience?

....
....

....
....

4. What reservations, if any, do you have about integrating a more holistic approach into your DBT practices? Are there any potential barriers you foresee?

....
....

....
....

5. How do you currently address the mind-body-emotion connection in therapy sessions? What strategies or interventions do you employ?

....
....

....
....

6. Reflect on your personal practices related to self-care and well-being. How do these practices influence your therapeutic approach, and in what ways might they align with holistic healing principles?

....
....

....
....

7. How do you currently gauge the success or effectiveness of your therapeutic interventions? Could a holistic approach offer additional metrics or indicators of client well-being?

....
....

....
....

8. In thinking about the broader landscape of mental health care, where do you see holistic healing fitting into future therapeutic practices?

....

....

....

....

9. What additional resources or training do you believe would benefit you most in integrating a holistic approach to DBT?

....

....

....

....

10. As you delve deeper into holistic healing, what do you hope to achieve for your clients and for your own professional growth?

....

....

....

....

Revisit these reflections periodically as you explore the integration of holistic methods with traditional DBT. They can serve as a touchstone, helping to guide your journey and track your evolution as a clinician.

Chapter 2: The Interdisciplinary Approach

Integrating Mindfulness, Somatic Techniques, and Cognitive Strategies

When clinicians harness the power of mindfulness, somatic techniques, and cognitive strategies together, they can offer a holistic healing experience that addresses the interconnectedness of the mind, body, and emotion. Each of these elements provides unique tools to manage distress and promote healing.

1. Mindfulness:

- **Definition:** Mindfulness refers to the practice of being present in the moment, observing thoughts, feelings, and bodily sensations without judgment.
- **Applications:**
    - **Observation without Judgment:** Clients learn to observe their thoughts and emotions as transient events, rather than absolute truths.
    - **Grounding Techniques:** Practices like the "5-4-3-2-1" sensory awareness exercise can help clients anchor themselves during moments of distress.

- **Meditation:** Guided or silent meditation sessions can cultivate a habit of centeredness and calm.

- **Benefits:** Mindfulness can reduce rumination, improve emotional regulation, increase self-awareness, and offer immediate relief during moments of acute stress.

2. Somatic Techniques:

- **Definition:** Somatic therapy emphasizes the connection between the mind and body. These techniques use the body to access layers of stored trauma and emotions, facilitating their release.

- **Applications:**

    - **Body Scanning:** Clients are guided to notice areas of tension or discomfort in their bodies, connecting these sensations with emotions or memories.

    - **Breathing Exercises:** Deep, intentional breathing can calm the nervous system, especially during panic or anxiety attacks.

    - **Movement Therapies:** This can include dance therapy, yoga, or tai chi, which encourage clients to express and process emotions through physical movement.

    - **Touch:** With appropriate boundaries and consent, therapeutic touch or tapping can help clients anchor themselves and process trauma.

- **Benefits:** Somatic techniques can help release stored trauma, improve the body's relaxation response, increase body awareness, and aid in grounding during dissociative episodes.

3. Cognitive Strategies:

- **Definition:** Cognitive strategies are rooted in the understanding that our thoughts, beliefs, and perceptions influence our emotions and behaviors.

- **Applications:**

    - **Cognitive Restructuring:** Clients learn to identify and challenge maladaptive thoughts, replacing them with more balanced or positive beliefs.

    - **Thought Stopping:** This technique helps clients interrupt and redirect harmful or obsessive thoughts.

    - **Problem-solving Therapy:** Clients are guided in identifying solutions to challenges, promoting a sense of agency and control.

    - **Journaling:** Writing can help clients process thoughts, notice patterns, and explore alternative perspectives.

- **Benefits:** Cognitive strategies can enhance problem-solving abilities, reduce the impact of negative thought patterns, increase self-awareness, and improve emotional regulation.

Integration of All Three Elements:

When combining mindfulness, somatic techniques, and cognitive strategies:

- **Session Flow:** A session might start with a mindfulness exercise to ground the client, followed by somatic exercises to release bodily tension, and then cognitive strategies to process the experience and reframe thoughts.

- **Homework Assignments:** Clients might be tasked with daily mindfulness practices, somatic exercises to notice body sensations throughout the day, and journaling exercises to reflect on their cognitive processes.

- **Deepened Awareness:** The combination allows for deeper awareness of how thoughts, emotions, and physical sensations influence each other, leading to more holistic insights and healing.

In conclusion, integrating mindfulness, somatic techniques, and cognitive strategies offers a robust, multifaceted approach to therapy. This holistic approach addresses the complexities of human experience, ensuring that clients are equipped with a diverse set of tools to navigate their healing journey.

Example 1: Overcoming Panic Attacks

- **Mindfulness:** During a session, a client feels the onset of a panic attack. The therapist guides them through a grounding exercise, asking them to focus on their breathing and take note of five things they can see, four they can touch, three they can hear, two they can smell, and one they can taste.
- **Somatic Technique:** After grounding with mindfulness, the therapist asks the client to place one hand on their chest and the other on their stomach, feeling the rise and fall as they breathe. This helps to connect the client to their body, drawing attention away from the spiraling panic and to the present physical moment.
- **Cognitive Strategy:** Once the immediate panic subsides, the therapist and client discuss the triggering thoughts. The client realizes they were ruminating on a past event. Together, they work on cognitive restructuring to challenge the negative

belief associated with that event, reframing it into a more neutral or positive perspective.

Example 2: Processing a Traumatic Memory

- **Mindfulness:** A client shares a traumatic memory. The therapist starts by guiding the client in a mindfulness meditation, focusing on the sensation of their feet touching the ground, ensuring they're present and grounded.
- **Somatic Technique:** The therapist observes that the client is holding tension in their shoulders and neck while discussing the trauma. The therapist guides the client in a body-scan exercise, identifying and releasing tension. This physical release can sometimes aid in releasing emotional tension related to the trauma.
- **Cognitive Strategy:** After processing the trauma, the therapist helps the client explore any self-blaming thoughts. They use cognitive strategies to challenge and reframe these thoughts, helping the client understand that they were not at fault.

Example 3: Addressing Chronic Negative Self-Talk

- **Mindfulness:** The client is asked to spend a few minutes each day noticing their self-talk without judgment. They simply observe the kind of language they use with themselves.

- **Somatic Technique:** During therapy, when the client shares a particularly harsh self-criticism, the therapist asks them to notice where they feel that statement in their body. Maybe it's a heaviness in the chest or a knot in the stomach. The therapist then guides the client through a breathing exercise, imagining sending breath to that area, helping dissipate the tension.
- **Cognitive Strategy:** The therapist and client work together to identify patterns in the negative self-talk. They then practice thought-stopping and replacement techniques. Every time the client notices a negative self-statement, they're taught to mentally "stop" and replace it with a pre-prepared positive affirmation.

In each example, the combination of mindfulness, somatic techniques, and cognitive strategies creates a comprehensive approach, addressing the issue from multiple angles and ensuring a deeper, holistic healing process.

Case Study 3

Case Study: The Transformation of Sarah's Therapy Session

Background:
Sarah, a 28-year-old graphic designer, had been attending therapy for major depressive disorder and generalized anxiety. She had experienced moderate success with traditional cognitive-behavioral therapy (CBT) techniques, but her progress had stagnated. Sarah often arrived at her sessions overwhelmed and found it challenging to articulate her feelings, which limited the effectiveness of talk-based interventions.

The Challenging Session:
During one particular session, Sarah entered visibly distressed. She had just received news of a close family member's sudden illness and was struggling to process her emotions. Her anxiety was heightened, and she appeared on the verge of a breakdown, unable to formulate sentences or express what she was feeling.

Interdisciplinary Approach to the Rescue:
Understanding the limitations of relying solely on talk-based interventions in this moment, her therapist decided to integrate a blend of mindfulness, somatic techniques, and cognitive strategies.

1. **Mindfulness:**

    - **Application:** The therapist began by guiding Sarah through a deep breathing exercise.

Asking her to close her eyes, focus on her breath, and feel the sensation of the air entering and leaving her nostrils. This provided immediate relief by drawing her attention away from the spiraling panic.

- **Outcome:** Sarah's breathing steadied, and she became more present, allowing for the next phase of the intervention.

2. **Somatic Technique:**

    - **Application:** Noticing that Sarah was clutching her chest, indicative of physical tension and distress, the therapist introduced a body-scan technique. Sarah was guided to mentally scan her body from head to toe, acknowledging areas of tension without trying to change them.

    - **Outcome:** By the end of the scan, Sarah's grip on her chest had loosened, her posture was more relaxed, and she conveyed a readiness to delve deeper into her feelings.

3. **Cognitive Strategy:**

    - **Application:** The therapist utilized a grounding technique, asking Sarah to describe five objects she could see in the room, trying to anchor her to the present. Once grounded, the therapist encouraged

Sarah to share her immediate thoughts about the family news, emphasizing that there were no right or wrong feelings.

- **Outcome:** Sarah began to articulate her fears about losing her family member, concerns about the future, and feelings of guilt for not being closer to home. With gentle prompting and challenging from the therapist, Sarah was able to reframe some of her guilt-driven beliefs, recognizing that she could not predict or control every life event.

Conclusion of the Session:
Thanks to the interdisciplinary approach, what started as an overwhelming session transformed into a productive exploration of deep-seated fears and beliefs. Sarah left feeling more grounded and with a set of tools to help navigate the difficult family situation ahead.

Long-Term Impact:
The success of this session became a turning point in Sarah's therapy. The therapist regularly integrated interdisciplinary techniques, ensuring Sarah was equipped to process emotions on multiple levels. Over time, Sarah reported increased emotional resilience, better stress management, and deeper insights into her mental health.

This case study underscores the power of an interdisciplinary approach, especially when traditional therapeutic models may fall short. The flexibility and depth of this method can make all the difference in challenging therapy sessions.

Reflection Space

Your Insights and Experiences:

This space is designed for you to capture any thoughts, feelings, insights, and experiences that arise as you engage with the material. The act of writing can help solidify your understanding, create personal connections to the content, and serve as a point of reference for future reflections.

Current Feelings:

How are you feeling in this moment as you engage with the content?

....
....

....
....

Key Insights:

What is one significant takeaway or "a-ha" moment you've had thus far?

....
....

....
....

Personal Application:

How do you see the material and concepts applying to your current professional situation?

....
....

....
....

Questions or Curiosities:

Are there any areas you're curious about or concepts you'd like to explore further?

....
....

....

....

Challenges and Reservations:

Are there any aspects of the content you find challenging or are hesitant about integrating into your practice?

....

....

....

....

Future Intentions:

What steps or strategies are you considering implementing in the near future based on your learnings?

....

....

....

....

Remember, these reflections are personal and for your benefit. It's okay if they evolve or change over time. Consider revisiting this space periodically as you delve deeper into the book to track your journey and growth as a clinician.

Chapter 3: Mindfulness Reimagined

Deepening the Mindfulness Practice

Mindfulness is the quality of being fully present, engaged in the here and now, without judgment. As one cultivates this practice, the depth of their connection to the present moment and their inner self can intensify. Deepening the mindfulness practice involves refining awareness, enhancing focus, and increasing the integration of mindfulness into daily life. Let's explore this journey.

1. Foundation of Mindfulness:

- **Beginner's Mind:** Approach experiences with openness and curiosity, as if you're encountering them for the first time. This perspective refreshes perception and reduces auto-pilot responses.
- **Non-judgmental Observation:** Recognize and acknowledge thoughts, feelings, and sensations without categorizing them as "good" or "bad." Instead, view them neutrally as passing events in consciousness.
- **Consistent Practice:** Start with short daily sessions of mindfulness meditation. The consistency of the practice is often more beneficial than its length.

2. Deepening Techniques:

- **Body Scan Meditation:** This involves moving focused attention through different parts of the body, usually starting from the toes and moving upwards. It cultivates both concentration and awareness of bodily sensations.
- **Loving-kindness Meditation (Metta):** This is a concentration practice where one generates feelings of goodwill and kindness towards themselves and others. It helps in developing compassion and reduces negative biases.
- **Walking Meditation:** Transform a simple act like walking into a mindful exercise, paying attention to every step and feeling the connection with the earth.

3. Expanding Awareness:

- **Open Monitoring:** Instead of focusing on one object of attention (like the breath), the practitioner remains open to whatever enters their field of consciousness. This expands awareness and enhances receptivity to the present moment.
- **Mindful Listening:** This practice involves fully attending to what another person is saying without forming reactive judgments or preparing a response. It enhances interpersonal relationships and reduces misunderstandings.

4. Integrating Mindfulness into Daily Activities:

- **Mindful Eating:** Instead of eating on autopilot, one fully savors every bite, noting the flavors, textures, and sensations of the food. This can transform a mundane task into a nourishing experience.

- **Mindful Breaks:** Incorporate short mindfulness sessions throughout the day, especially during work. A few minutes of deep breathing or focusing on ambient sounds can recharge the mind.

5. Embracing Challenges:

- **Mindfulness in Difficult Times:** Instead of avoiding discomfort or challenging emotions, use mindfulness to lean into them with curiosity. This can reveal deeper insights and promote emotional resilience.

- **Awareness of Habitual Patterns:** With deepened mindfulness, one starts noticing recurring mental patterns or habits. Recognizing them is the first step towards transformation.

6. Joining a Mindful Community:

- **Group Meditations:** Practicing with others can amplify motivation and provide a space for shared experiences and learning.

- **Retreats:** Participating in longer meditation retreats can intensify the practice and offer a deeper dive into mindfulness.

Conclusion:

Deepening the mindfulness practice is not just about enhancing concentration but about integrating mindfulness into every facet of life. As one advances, the boundaries between formal mindfulness practice and daily activities start to blur. This integrated approach promotes a life lived fully in the present, imbued with clarity, compassion, and wisdom.

Case Study 4

Case Study: Maya's Journey to Deeper Healing with Enhanced Mindfulness Techniques

Background:

Maya, a 35-year-old project manager, initially sought therapy due to persistent feelings of burnout, stress, and a sense of disconnection from herself and others. While she had some prior exposure to basic mindfulness practices, such as brief guided meditations through mobile apps, she had never integrated them into her daily life consistently.

The Initial Phase:

Maya's therapist introduced her to foundational mindfulness practices, emphasizing consistent daily meditation. Initially, Maya found the practice to be calming, particularly in stressful situations. However, she admitted feeling as if she was just "scratching the surface" and yearned for a deeper connection.

Deepening the Practice:

1. **Body Scan Meditation:** To cultivate a stronger connection with her body, Maya began practicing body scan meditation. This not only improved her focus but also made her more aware of the physical manifestations of her stress, such as tightness in her chest and shoulders.

2. **Open Monitoring:** Transitioning from focused attention on her breath, Maya was guided to observe all sensations, thoughts, and emotions without attachment. This practice uncovered buried emotions and memories, which became pivotal discussion points in her therapy sessions.

3. **Mindful Listening:** To address her feelings of disconnection from others, Maya was encouraged to practice mindful listening. Over time, she reported improved relationships, particularly with her partner and colleagues, as she became a more attentive and empathetic listener.

Challenges and Breakthroughs:

As Maya delved deeper into these practices, she encountered emotional challenges. Open monitoring, in particular, brought forth unresolved childhood traumas.

Instead of avoiding these memories, Maya, with the support of her therapist, used her honed mindfulness skills to approach them with curiosity and compassion.

Integrating Mindfulness into Daily Life:

Maya began to incorporate mindfulness into daily activities. Mindful eating transformed her previously rushed lunches into moments of genuine pleasure and gratitude. Mindful breaks at work, even if just for a few minutes, significantly reduced her feelings of burnout.

Joining a Mindful Community:

On her therapist's recommendation, Maya joined a local meditation group. This community provided her with a space to share her experiences and challenges, amplifying her motivation and commitment.

Outcome:

A year into her deepened mindfulness journey, Maya expressed a profound shift in her life. She felt more connected to her emotions, her body, and the people around her. She learned to approach life's challenges with a balanced perspective and found joy in everyday moments that she had previously overlooked.

Conclusion:

Maya's experience underscores the transformative potential of deepening the mindfulness practice. While foundational techniques provided initial relief, it was the advanced practices, integrated into her daily life and supported by therapy and community, that facilitated profound healing and personal growth.

Reflection Space

This reflection space is designed to guide you in introspection about your current mindfulness teaching methodologies. As you progress in your role as a facilitator, revisiting and refining your approach is essential for ensuring the most impactful and beneficial experience for your clients.

Current Techniques:

List the mindfulness techniques you currently teach or recommend most frequently.

....
....

....
....

Success Stories:

Recall a recent instance where a client benefited significantly from a mindfulness technique. What was the technique, and why was it effective?

....
....

....

....

Challenges in Teaching:

What obstacles or resistance have you encountered when introducing mindfulness to clients?

....

....

....

....

Adaptations and Customizations:

Describe a situation where you had to adapt or modify a traditional mindfulness practice to better suit a client's needs.

....

....

....

....

Personal Practice:

Reflect on your mindfulness routine. How often do you practice? Which techniques do you gravitate towards, and why?

....

....

....

....

Continuous Learning:

Are there any advanced mindfulness practices or concepts you're curious to explore or integrate into your teaching?

....

....

....

....

Feedback and Iteration:

How do you gather feedback from clients on the effectiveness of the mindfulness techniques taught? How do you implement changes based on this feedback?

....

....

....

....

Vision for the Future:

As you look forward in your role as a mindfulness facilitator, what are your goals? How do you envision deepening and expanding your teaching techniques?

....
....

....
....

The journey of teaching and guiding others in mindfulness is an evolving process. Regular reflection on your methods and openness to adaptation will ensure that you remain effective and relevant in the ever-changing landscape of therapeutic techniques.

Chapter 4: Somatic Techniques for Emotional Regulation

Introduction to Somatic Healing

Somatic healing is based on the understanding that the body and mind are intricately linked and that trauma, stress, and emotional experiences manifest not just mentally, but also physically within the body. The word "somatic" comes from the Greek word "soma," which means the living body in its wholeness. Thus, somatic healing aims to address both the body and mind to bring about holistic recovery and wellness.

1. Historical Context and Evolution:

Historically, many ancient cultures recognized the interconnectedness of body and mind. From traditional Chinese medicine to Ayurveda in India, the body has been seen as a reflection of mental, emotional, and spiritual states. In modern times, the formal recognition of somatic practices emerged in the late 19th and early 20th centuries with the advent of somatic psychology.

2. The Body-Mind Connection:

The fundamental premise of somatic healing is that our bodies store memories, emotions, and traumas. For instance, someone who has experienced a traumatic event may carry residual tension, often unconsciously, in specific body parts like the shoulders or the stomach. Over time, these physical manifestations can result in chronic pain, posture problems, or other health issues.

3. Techniques and Practices:

There are various somatic healing techniques designed to help individuals reconnect with their bodies, release stored tension, and reprocess traumatic experiences. Some prominent techniques include:

- **Somatic Experiencing:** Developed by Dr. Peter Levine, this approach is focused on releasing the energy trapped in the body following trauma. It involves tracking bodily sensations and guiding individuals to move through stuck patterns.
- **Bioenergetics:** Founded by Alexander Lowen, this technique uses exercises to release tension in the body and promote emotional expression.
- **Bodywork and Touch:** Techniques such as massage therapy, Rolfing, or craniosacral therapy aim to manipulate and heal the body's physical structures, often releasing emotional traumas in the process.
- **Movement Therapies:** Methods like dance therapy or Feldenkrais use movement to improve self-awareness, expression, and healing.

4. Benefits of Somatic Healing:

- **Release of Stored Trauma:** By addressing trauma stored in the body, individuals often find relief from chronic pain, tension, or other physical ailments.
- **Enhanced Emotional Processing:** Physical interventions can serve as a conduit for processing and understanding emotions.
- **Improved Body Awareness:** Individuals become more attuned to their bodies' signals, allowing for better self-regulation and care.
- **Holistic Wellness:** By addressing both mental and physical components of well-being, somatic healing promotes holistic health and resilience.

5. Integrating Somatic Healing with Other Therapies:

Given its focus on the body-mind connection, somatic healing can seamlessly integrate with other therapeutic modalities like cognitive-behavioral therapy, mindfulness, or traditional talk therapy. This interdisciplinary approach ensures that individuals receive a comprehensive healing experience.

Conclusion:

Somatic healing underscores the profound connection between our physical bodies and our emotional and mental states. By addressing this interconnectedness, individuals can find deeper healing, transcending the limitations of therapies that focus solely on the mind or the body. As research continues and awareness grows, the potential of somatic healing in transforming lives is becoming increasingly evident.

Case Study 5

Case Study: Nina's Path to Emotional Regulation through Bodywork Techniques

Background:

Nina, a 28-year-old graphic designer, initially came to therapy due to recurring panic attacks and pervasive feelings of anxiety that she found challenging to manage through traditional cognitive interventions. Despite making some progress with talk therapy, she felt something was missing, often describing an "unseen weight" she carried in her chest and back.

The Discovery Phase:

During one session, while discussing a particularly stressful event, Nina's therapist observed her subconsciously rubbing her temples and clenching her jaw. Recognizing the potential somatic connection, the therapist introduced the idea of integrating bodywork techniques to complement their current therapeutic approach.

Introducing Bodywork:

1. **Craniosacral Therapy:** Nina began with craniosacral therapy, a gentle hands-on technique that focuses on the bones of the head, spinal column, and sacrum. Over several sessions, Nina reported a noticeable reduction in her headaches and a greater sense of calm.

2. **Deep Tissue Massage:** To address the tension in her shoulders and back, Nina underwent a series of deep tissue massages. These not only alleviated her physical discomfort but also triggered emotional releases. During one session, she remembered a childhood incident that had led her to adopt a protective, hunched posture.

3. **Myofascial Release:** This technique, focusing on releasing muscular shortness and tightness, further assisted Nina in loosening the physical "armor" she had built up over the years.

Connecting Physical and Emotional Releases:

As Nina began to release physical tension, she noticed her emotional landscape shifting as well. The heavy weight in her chest started to dissipate. After one particularly intense massage session, Nina experienced a flood of emotions, ranging from grief to relief, and subsequently had a breakthrough in discussing previously unexplored traumatic experiences.

Incorporating Self-Regulation Techniques:

Nina was taught to recognize her body's stress signals and use self-massage and stretching as immediate interventions. By learning to soothe herself physically, she found it easier to manage her emotional reactions. This combination of bodywork and self-awareness equipped Nina with a tangible toolkit to combat her anxiety.

Outcome:

After six months of integrating bodywork techniques with traditional therapy, Nina reported a dramatic reduction in her panic attacks. The feeling of an "unseen weight" had largely dissipated. She felt more in tune with her body, enabling her to preemptively address signs of stress before they escalated into anxiety or panic.

Conclusion:

Nina's journey highlights the profound connection between the physical body and emotional well-being. By addressing and releasing stored physical tension, she was able to unlock deeper emotional healing, showcasing the transformative potential of an integrated therapeutic approach.

Reflection Space

Taking a moment to introspect can often illuminate our beliefs, biases, and curiosities. As you delve into the world of somatic healing and its techniques, this space is designed for you to pause, contemplate, and document your insights.

Initial Reactions:

After reading about somatic healing and its techniques, what are your immediate thoughts or feelings?

....
....

....
....

Personal Resonance:

Can you identify any personal experiences where your body reacted to emotional stress or trauma?

....
....

....
....

Potential Benefits:

How do you envision somatic techniques benefiting your clients or enhancing your current therapeutic approaches?

....
....

....
....

Barriers and Concerns:

Are there any apprehensions or barriers you perceive in integrating somatic techniques into your practice?

....
....

....
....

Desire for Training:

How inclined are you to pursue further training or education in specific somatic techniques? Which ones intrigue you the most?

....
....

....
....

Feedback from Clients:

If you have already integrated any somatic techniques, how have clients responded? What feedback or observations stand out?

....
....

....
....

Vision for Integration:

In an ideal scenario, how would you seamlessly integrate somatic healing with other therapeutic modalities? What would that look like in a session?

....
....

....
....

Remember, the field of psychotherapy is vast and ever-evolving. Somatic techniques offer one pathway among many to foster deep healing. Whether you decide to incorporate them or not, understanding their principles and potential can only enrich your therapeutic toolbox. Always keep an open mind, continue to learn, and choose the best paths tailored for each individual's journey toward healing.

Chapter 5: Cognitive Strategies and the Holistic Model

Expanding Cognitive Strategies with a Holistic Focus

Cognitive strategies, which stem primarily from Cognitive Behavioral Therapy (CBT), traditionally focus on identifying and restructuring maladaptive thoughts to bring about emotional and behavioral change. However, if we're to offer a more encompassing healing approach, it becomes necessary to weave in elements that speak to the entirety of a person's experience – mind, body, and spirit. This holistic focus allows us to address not just the cognitive aspects but the entire ecosystem in which thoughts are formed and manifested.

1. Understanding the Limitations of Traditional Cognitive Strategies:

While CBT has been remarkably effective for many, there's growing recognition that thoughts don't exist in a vacuum. They're influenced by bodily sensations, external environments, cultural backgrounds, and deeper, sometimes spiritual, beliefs about the world.

2. Body Awareness and Cognitive Processes:

Our bodies provide a continuous stream of feedback about our environment and internal state. By becoming more attuned to this feedback:

- **Somatic Cognitions:** Recognize that certain thoughts are often accompanied by specific bodily sensations. For instance, the thought "I'm not good enough" might manifest as a sinking feeling in the stomach.
- **Feedback Loops:** By addressing the physical manifestation of a thought, we can influence the thought itself. Deep breathing or grounding exercises, when feeling overwhelmed, can modulate the intensity and frequency of anxiety-provoking thoughts.

3. Incorporating Mindfulness into Cognitive Strategies:

Mindfulness, the act of being present without judgment, can enhance cognitive strategies:

- **Thought Observation:** Instead of immediately challenging a negative thought, one can first observe it non-judgmentally, understanding its transient nature.
- **Emotional Detachment:** This allows individuals to see thoughts as mere mental events, reducing the emotional impact of negative cognitions.

4. Cultural and Environmental Considerations:

To have a holistic cognitive approach, understanding an individual's cultural and environmental context is crucial:

- **Cultural Beliefs:** Recognize how certain cultural beliefs influence thoughts and feelings. A holistic approach might involve integrating these beliefs in a way that's healing rather than detrimental.
- **Environmental Impact:** Acknowledging the influence of one's environment – whether it's a bustling city or a serene countryside – on cognitive processes.

5. Spirituality and Cognition:

For many, spirituality provides a foundational framework for understanding the world:

- **Integrating Spiritual Beliefs:** If a client holds certain spiritual beliefs, these can be woven into cognitive restructuring. For example, if someone believes in the idea of destiny, challenging a negative thought might involve exploring this concept in a supportive manner.
- **Meditative and Reflective Practices:** These can be integrated to deepen cognitive work, allowing for introspection at a level that traditional strategies might not reach.

6. Holistic Techniques to Enhance Cognitive Work:

- **Visualization Techniques:** Going beyond mere thought restructuring, one could visualize a positive outcome or memory, engaging all senses.

- **Narrative Therapy Elements:** Exploring a person's life story in depth can provide context to certain entrenched beliefs and offer avenues to reframe them.

Conclusion:

Expanding cognitive strategies with a holistic focus ensures that the therapeutic process is more encompassing. By weaving in elements of body awareness, mindfulness, cultural considerations, and spirituality, clinicians can offer a richer, multi-dimensional approach to healing that respects and addresses the entirety of an individual's experience.

Case Study 6

Case Study: The Transformation of Alex through Holistic Cognitive Strategy

Background:

Alex, a 35-year-old software engineer, had been in therapy for years to address recurring feelings of inadequacy and imposter syndrome, especially in his professional life. Despite understanding the irrationality of his beliefs through traditional cognitive strategies, he struggled to truly break free from these entrenched thought patterns.

Presenting Issue:

Every time Alex was presented with a new project or task at work, he was plagued by thoughts like, "I won't be able to handle this," "Others are better than me," and "I'll be exposed as a fraud." Even after numerous achievements, these thoughts persisted.

The Holistic Turnaround:

1. **Body Awareness:** Alex's therapist noticed that every time they discussed work-related matters, Alex would become tense, especially around his shoulders and neck. Through guided body-awareness exercises, Alex learned to identify and then release this physical tension, which helped him approach his thought patterns with more clarity and calmness.

2. **Mindfulness Integration:** Rather than immediately trying to challenge or change his thoughts, Alex was taught to simply observe them. This non-judgmental approach allowed him to see these beliefs as fleeting thoughts rather than truths. Over time, this reduced the intensity of his negative reactions.

3. **Cultural and Environmental Exploration:** Delving into Alex's background, it was revealed that growing up in a highly competitive educational environment had ingrained these feelings of never being "good enough." By addressing these foundational experiences and understanding their context, Alex started viewing his current challenges through a more compassionate lens.

4. **Spiritual Reconnection:** Alex had a latent belief in the universe having a plan for everyone. His therapist used this to help him reframe his challenges as lessons or milestones in his life journey, changing the narrative from being "not good enough" to "learning and evolving."

5. **Visualization Technique:** Alex was encouraged to visualize himself successfully completing projects and being acknowledged for his skills. This not only boosted his confidence but also started to reshape his inner narrative.

6. **Engaging with Nature:** Recognizing the calming effect nature had on Alex, his therapist suggested regular walks in the park. Over time, this acted as a grounding exercise that helped him disconnect from spiraling thoughts.

Breakthrough:

During a particularly challenging project at work, Alex felt the familiar wave of doubt and anxiety. However, this time, instead of succumbing to it, he employed the techniques he learned. He took a short break, went for a walk outside, practiced some grounding exercises, and visualized a successful outcome. When he returned, he tackled the project with renewed vigor and confidence.

Conclusion:

For Alex, traditional cognitive strategies provided insight but not the breakthrough he needed. By adopting a holistic approach that combined body awareness, mindfulness, spiritual beliefs, and a deeper understanding of his past, he was able to truly shift his perspective. This case underscores the potential of holistic cognitive strategies to bring about profound change, even when traditional methods seem to reach a standstill.

Reflection Space

Reflection Space: Integrating Holistic Cognitive Strategies

As you journey through the world of holistic cognitive strategies, it's essential to periodically pause, assimilate, and reflect. This reflection space provides structured prompts to help you delve deeper into your understanding and contemplate the application of these strategies in your therapeutic practice.

Your Foundations:

How do you currently perceive and utilize cognitive strategies in your practice?

....
....

....
....

Body Awareness:

Have you noticed any physical reactions in your clients that correlate with specific thought patterns or emotions? How might you incorporate body awareness exercises to address these?

....
....

....
....

The Role of Mindfulness:

Reflect on a session where integrating mindfulness might have offered a different perspective or outcome for your client. How would you have incorporated it?

....
....

....
....

Cultural and Environmental Influences:

Can you recall an instance where a client's cultural or environmental background heavily influenced their thought patterns? How did you address it, and how might a holistic approach refine your response in the future?

....
....

……………………………………………………………………………………
……………………

Spirituality in Therapy:

How comfortable are you in addressing and integrating spiritual beliefs into cognitive strategies? Do you see potential benefits or challenges?

……………………………………………………………………………………
……………………

……………………………………………………………………………………
……………………

Visualization and Other Techniques:

Think about a time when a client struggled to change a negative belief. How might visualization or narrative therapy have provided a breakthrough?

……………………………………………………………………………………
……………………

……………………………………………………………………………………
……………………

Personal Growth:

As a clinician, in what areas do you feel you need more training or understanding to effectively integrate holistic cognitive strategies?

....
....

....
....

Every therapist's journey is unique. The aim is not to overhaul your existing methods but to enhance them, offering clients a comprehensive approach that resonates with their individual experiences. By continually reflecting and adapting, you enrich not only your clients' therapeutic experience but also your own professional growth.

Chapter 6: Putting It All Together - A Holistic DBT Session

The Flow of an Interdisciplinary Session

Interdisciplinary sessions blend multiple therapeutic modalities to provide a holistic approach to treatment. These sessions can be incredibly rewarding, offering clients a multi-faceted healing experience. However, orchestrating a session that seamlessly integrates various techniques requires careful planning and flexibility. Here's a generalized flow of how an interdisciplinary session might be conducted:

1. Setting the Ground:

- **Establish the Intention:** Begin by understanding and setting the intention for the session. What does the client hope to achieve? This will guide which techniques are chosen and how they're integrated.

- **Mindful Beginning:** Start the session with a short mindfulness exercise, allowing the client to become present, grounding them in the here and now.

2. Cognitive Processing:

- **Discuss the Presenting Issue:** Allow the client to talk about the main issue or challenge they're facing. This helps in understanding their cognitive patterns and initial emotional responses.

- **Cognitive Reframing:** Introduce cognitive strategies to challenge and reframe maladaptive thoughts. This can include techniques from Cognitive Behavioral Therapy (CBT) or other cognitive-based modalities.

3. Dive Deeper with Somatic Exploration:

- **Body Scan:** Conduct a brief body scan, encouraging the client to recognize any physical sensations or tensions associated with their emotions or thoughts. This somatic check-in helps in addressing stored trauma or stress in the body.

- **Somatic Interventions:** Depending on the client's comfort and the therapist's expertise, use somatic techniques such as breathwork, grounding exercises, or even gentle movement to help release and process these sensations.

4. Emotional Processing:

- **Emotion-focused Techniques:** Explore the emotional dimensions of the client's issue. Techniques from Emotion-Focused Therapy (EFT) or Gestalt therapy can be employed to deepen emotional understanding and processing.

- **Expression and Validation:** Create a space where the client can freely express their emotions and feel validated in their experience.

5. Integration of Insights:

- **Mind-Body Connection:** Discuss insights from both cognitive and somatic exploration. How do thoughts influence physical sensations and vice versa?

- **Personal Narrative:** If suitable, engage the client in narrative therapy elements, helping them re-author their story with new insights and experiences from the session.

6. Techniques for Continuation:

- **Skill Building:** Introduce or reinforce specific skills the client can practice between sessions. This can include mindfulness exercises, cognitive reframing techniques, or simple somatic practices.

7. Closing the Session:

- **Feedback Loop:** Create a space for the client to share their experience of the interdisciplinary session. What resonated with them? What was challenging?

- **Grounding Exercise:** End with another grounding exercise, ensuring the client feels stable and present before leaving the session.

- **Setting Intentions for Next Session:** Briefly discuss potential focus areas or techniques to explore in the next session, giving the client a sense of continuity and purpose.

Note: It's essential to remember that the interdisciplinary approach requires flexibility. Not every session will incorporate all elements, and the therapist must remain attuned to the client's needs, pacing the session according to their comfort and receptivity. The aim is to offer a harmonious blend of modalities that holistically address mind, body, and emotion.

Case Study 7

Case Study: The Interdisciplinary Journey of Sarah

Background: Sarah, a 28-year-old marketing executive, presented with feelings of burnout, recurrent anxiety, and bouts of inexplicable sadness. Although successful in her career, she constantly felt overwhelmed and dissatisfied.

1. Setting the Ground:

Establishing the Intention: Sarah wanted clarity on her overwhelming feelings and sought strategies to handle her stress better.

Mindful Beginning: The therapist initiated a 5-minute guided meditation, focusing on Sarah's breath, to help her transition from her hectic day into the session.

2. Cognitive Processing:

Discussing the Presenting Issue: Sarah shared her recent challenges, mentioning her constant fear of underperforming at work and her persistent feeling of not being "good enough."

Cognitive Reframing: The therapist introduced the concept of cognitive distortions, helping Sarah identify her patterns of "all-or-nothing thinking" and "personalization."

3. Dive Deeper with Somatic Exploration:

Body Scan: Sarah was guided to notice sensations in her body. She felt a heaviness in her chest and tension in her shoulders.

Somatic Interventions: The therapist led Sarah in a deep breathing exercise, focusing on expanding the chest and releasing shoulder tension. After a few minutes, Sarah reported a decrease in the heaviness she felt.

4. Emotional Processing:

Emotion-focused Techniques: Using a technique from Emotion-Focused Therapy, Sarah was asked to "sit" with the feeling of not being good enough and converse with it.

Through this, Sarah unearthed memories of academic pressure from her childhood.

Expression and Validation: Sarah expressed feelings of sadness and anger towards her younger self, with the therapist validating her emotions and ensuring she felt heard.

5. Integration of Insights:

Mind-Body Connection: Sarah and the therapist discussed the physical sensations associated with her memories and feelings, highlighting the strong interplay between thoughts, emotions, and bodily sensations.

Personal Narrative: Sarah was guided to reframe her story, focusing on her resilience and growth instead of solely her challenges.

6. Techniques for Continuation:

Skill Building: Sarah was introduced to the "STOP" technique for moments of overwhelming anxiety:

- **S**top what you're doing.
- **T**ake a few deep breaths.
- **O**bserve your thoughts, emotions, and physical sensations.

- **P**roceed with an action that supports your current needs.

7. Closing the Session:

Feedback Loop: Sarah shared that the session felt comprehensive, and she was particularly amazed by the immediate relief the somatic exercises provided.

Grounding Exercise: A brief visualization exercise was conducted, imagining a protective bubble around her, to ensure Sarah felt secure and anchored.

Setting Intentions for Next Session: The therapist and Sarah agreed to delve deeper into her childhood experiences, potentially integrating art therapy techniques to aid her exploration.

Conclusion: This session epitomized the integrative potential of an interdisciplinary approach. Sarah not only gained cognitive insights but also experienced emotional release and somatic relief. The session laid the foundation for her continued therapeutic journey, emphasizing the harmony between mind, body, and emotion.

Reflection Space

Reflection Space: Crafting Your Holistic Session

As you've journeyed through the interdisciplinary landscapes of therapy, it's now time to envision your own holistic session. This reflection space provides structured prompts to help you design a unique, integrative therapeutic experience for your clients.

Envisioning the Client

Think of a current or hypothetical client. What are their presenting issues?

....
....

....
....

Setting the Stage

How will you create a welcoming and grounding environment at the beginning of the session? Consider both the physical space and initial interactions.

....
....

....
....

Cognitive Exploration:

Which cognitive techniques might be beneficial for this client? How can you weave them into the session to address their specific concerns?

....
....

....
....

Somatic Integration

Based on the client's issues and comfort level, which somatic techniques might be beneficial? How can you help them connect their bodily sensations with their thoughts and emotions?

....
....

....
....

Emotional Journey:

Envision the emotional depth you'd like to explore. Which techniques or exercises can help the client process and express their emotions?

....
....

....

....

Integrative Insights:

How will you help the client tie together the insights from the cognitive, somatic, and emotional exploration? Think of tools or discussions that might aid this integration.

....

....

....

....

Skill Building & Takeaways:

What specific skills or techniques would you like the client to practice or reflect on after the session?

....

....

....

....

Feedback & Closure:

How will you ensure the session ends on a positive, grounding note? How might you gather feedback to inform future sessions?

....
....

....
....

Personal Reflection:

What challenges do you anticipate in conducting such a session? What areas do you feel you need to study further or seek supervision in?

....
....

....
....

Remember, crafting an interdisciplinary session is both an art and a science. It's about understanding the intricate dance between various therapeutic modalities and the unique rhythm of each client. As you envision and plan, be open to adapting, learning, and growing in your holistic therapeutic journey.

Chapter 7: Challenges in Integrating a Holistic Approach

Addressing Skepticism

Skepticism is a natural and often necessary stance individuals may take when confronted with new information, techniques, or modalities, especially in fields like psychotherapy. Skepticism can arise from practitioners, clients, or even the wider community. Addressing it is crucial for fostering trust, building credibility, and facilitating effective therapeutic interventions.

1. Understanding the Root of Skepticism:

Before you can address skepticism, it's vital to understand where it's coming from:

- **Previous Negative Experiences:** Someone may have had an unsatisfactory or even harmful experience with a particular modality or practitioner in the past.
- **Cultural or Societal Beliefs:** Certain cultures or societies might view certain therapeutic practices with suspicion due to longstanding traditions or beliefs.
- **Fear of the Unknown:** Anything new or unfamiliar can be intimidating or unsettling.

- **Scientific Rigor:** A lack of substantial empirical evidence supporting a particular method can result in skepticism, especially among scientifically-minded individuals.

2. Providing Evidence:

Wherever possible, back up claims with empirical evidence:

- **Research Studies:** Share studies or meta-analyses that support the efficacy of the approach you're recommending.
- **Case Studies:** Real-life examples can be powerful in showcasing how a particular modality has helped others in similar situations.
- **Professional Endorsements:** Recommendations or endorsements from reputable professionals or institutions can lend credibility.

3. Building Trust and Rapport:

Fostering a therapeutic alliance is fundamental:

- **Open Dialogue:** Create a safe space where clients or skeptics can express their concerns and ask questions without fear of judgment.
- **Transparency:** Be open about the methods you're using, their origins, and their intended benefits.

- **Empathy:** Be understanding and compassionate towards the individual's doubts or concerns.

4. Educating and Informing:

Awareness is a potent antidote to skepticism:

- **Workshops and Seminars:** Host informational sessions about the therapeutic modality in question.
- **Resources:** Provide books, articles, or other materials that explain and validate the approach.
- **Demonstrations:** For some, seeing is believing. Offering demonstrations can demystify the process.

5. Respecting Autonomy:

Recognize that not every method will resonate with every individual:

- **Choice:** Offer clients the opportunity to choose or integrate different therapeutic modalities based on their comfort level.
- **Flexibility:** Adapt your approach based on feedback and the individual's evolving needs or beliefs.
- **No Pressure:** It's essential to avoid pressuring anyone into a particular method or technique.

6. Continued Learning and Adaptation:

Stay updated with the latest in therapeutic research and practice:

- **Professional Development:** Attend trainings, workshops, and conferences to continue honing your skills and knowledge.
- **Feedback Loop:** Regularly seek feedback from clients or peers to refine your approach and address any arising skepticism more effectively.

Skepticism isn't necessarily negative. It can push professionals to provide the best, most evidence-based care possible. By addressing skepticism with empathy, evidence, and education, practitioners can bridge gaps in understanding and pave the way for more holistic, integrated healing experiences.

Case Study 8

Case Study: Embracing Holistic Healing Amidst Doubt

Background:

Name: Maya

Age: 34

Presenting Issue: Chronic insomnia compounded by increasing anxiety about sleep. Previous therapeutic interventions provided only short-term relief.

The Holistic Approach:

Given Maya's lack of sustained relief from traditional interventions, her therapist, Dr. Rivera, suggested a holistic approach integrating mindfulness, somatic techniques, and cognitive strategies.

1. **Mindfulness:** Guided meditation to cultivate present-moment awareness.
2. **Somatic Techniques:** Progressive muscle relaxation to reduce physical tension before sleep.
3. **Cognitive Strategies:** Cognitive Behavioral Therapy for Insomnia (CBT-I) techniques.

Challenges:

1. **Initial Skepticism:** Maya doubted the efficacy of meditation. Having come from a pragmatic background, she considered mindfulness and body-focused techniques "new age" and potentially ineffective.
2. **Physical Discomfort:** The somatic techniques, initially, heightened Maya's awareness of her physical discomfort, making her more restless.
3. **Emotional Resurgence:** Mindfulness practices made Maya more aware of suppressed emotions, leading to initial increases in nighttime anxiety.

Overcoming the Challenges:

1. **Education and Transparency:** Dr. Rivera provided Maya with empirical studies showing the benefits of mindfulness and somatic techniques on insomnia and anxiety. By showcasing evidence and explaining the science behind each method, Dr. Rivera bridged Maya's initial skepticism.

2. **Modified Techniques:** Seeing Maya's discomfort with certain somatic exercises, Dr. Rivera introduced gentle yoga stretches tailored to Maya's comfort and physical capacity. These served as a gentle introduction to body awareness.

3. **Phased Integration:** Instead of simultaneous introduction, Dr. Rivera sequenced the modalities. They began with CBT-I to address immediate sleep-related cognitions. Once Maya experienced some relief, they introduced mindfulness to help with emotional regulation, followed by somatic techniques for relaxation.

4. **Continuous Feedback:** Dr. Rivera ensured open communication, allowing Maya to express any concerns or discomforts. This helped in tailoring the techniques to Maya's evolving needs.

5. **Supplementary Resources:** Maya was given access to books, podcasts, and apps that reinforced the holistic approach's concepts. Familiarizing herself

with these outside of sessions made her more receptive during therapy.

Outcome:

After several sessions and with a paced, respectful approach to Maya's skepticism, she began to experience the benefits. She reported improved sleep quality and a noticeable reduction in nighttime anxiety. Moreover, Maya expressed gratitude for the new tools she had gained, which helped her not just with her sleep, but in managing stress in various areas of her life.

Conclusion:

Maya's journey underscores the importance of patience, flexibility, and evidence-based communication in holistic therapy. Challenges, especially with non-traditional methods, are inevitable. However, with a dedicated, empathetic approach, even the most skeptical clients can reap the profound benefits of an integrated healing journey.

Reflection Space

Reflection Space: Anticipating and Navigating Challenges in Holistic Therapy

Holistic therapy's interdisciplinary nature brings a depth of healing potential. Still, it also introduces its unique set of challenges. Reflecting on these beforehand prepares you to navigate them with grace and confidence. Use this space to anticipate potential hurdles and brainstorm ways to handle them.

1. **Foreseeable Challenges:**

Think about the holistic techniques you're considering integrating. What resistance or challenges might you anticipate from clients, peers, or even yourself?

Potential Challenge 1:

....
....

Potential Challenge 2:

....
....

Potential Challenge 3:

....
....

2. **Navigating Skepticism:**

It's natural for new or unfamiliar techniques to face skepticism. How might you address doubts or concerns from clients or colleagues?

Strategy 1:

....
....

Strategy 2:

....
....

3. Ensuring Comfort & Safety:

Considering the somatic and emotional depth of holistic therapy, how can you ensure your client feels safe and comfortable throughout the process?

Comfort Measure 1:

....
....

Comfort Measure 2:

....
....

4. Tailoring Techniques:

Each client is unique. How can you adapt holistic techniques to individual needs, comfort levels, or potential traumas?

Adaptation Strategy 1:

....
....

Adaptation Strategy 2:

....

....

5. **Personal Reflection:**

Reflect on your own readiness and comfort in integrating holistic techniques. What further training, education, or self-awareness practices might you need?

Personal Development Area 1:

....

....

Personal Development Area 2:

....

....

As you fill out this reflection space, remember that challenges are inherent in growth. They offer opportunities for learning, adaptation, and deepened connection with clients. Regularly revisiting and updating this reflection can provide a valuable roadmap as you further your journey into holistic healing.

Chapter 8: Measuring Outcomes and Success

Evidence-Based Benefits of a Holistic Approach

Holistic approaches in therapeutic contexts are grounded in the belief that individuals are more than just the sum of their parts and that optimal health and well-being result from the harmonious functioning of physical, psychological, social, and spiritual aspects. Over the years, research has increasingly validated the benefits of holistic interventions in various fields of health and well-being. Here are some of the evidence-based benefits of a holistic approach:

1. **Enhanced Mental Health:**

    - Holistic practices such as mindfulness meditation have been shown to reduce symptoms of anxiety, depression, and PTSD. For instance, meta-analyses of mindfulness-based therapy have shown significant benefits for anxiety and mood symptoms in clinical populations.

2. **Improved Physical Health:**

    - Somatic therapies, like yoga and tai chi, have demonstrated improvements in cardiovascular health, immune function, and pain reduction. A systematic review and meta-analysis of randomized controlled trials found that yoga improves several cardiovascular risk factors in patients with metabolic syndrome and high cardiovascular risk.

3. **Stress Reduction:**

    - Techniques like deep breathing exercises, progressive muscle relaxation, and guided imagery have been proven to lower cortisol levels, the body's primary stress hormone.

4. **Enhanced Cognitive Function:**

    - Mindfulness and meditation practices have been linked to improvements in attention, memory, and cognitive flexibility. A study in the journal Psychological Science found that participating in an intensive meditation training program led to improvements in mood, visuo-spatial processing, working memory, and cognitive flexibility.

5. **Holistic Pain Management:**

    - Integrative therapies such as acupuncture, massage therapy, and certain herbal treatments have demonstrated effectiveness in pain management, potentially reducing the need for pharmacological interventions.

6. **Improved Emotional Regulation:**

    - Emotion-focused holistic therapies can provide tools and strategies to help individuals understand, express, and regulate their emotions, leading to more balanced and adaptive emotional responses.

7. **Enhancement of Personal Awareness and Growth:**

    - Holistic practices often encourage introspection and self-awareness, fostering a deeper understanding of oneself, promoting personal growth and enhancing self-acceptance.

8. **Better Interpersonal Relationships:**

    - By fostering self-awareness, empathy, and effective communication skills, holistic therapies can lead to healthier interpersonal dynamics.

9. **Integration of Mind-Body Connection:**

    - Somatic techniques can help individuals reconnect with their bodies, recognize physical manifestations of emotional distress, and use the body as a tool for healing. Research has highlighted that somatic experiencing can be effective in treating trauma and stressor-related disorders.

10. **Improved Quality of Life:**

- By addressing not just symptoms but the entirety of an individual's experience, holistic therapies often lead to improvements in overall well-being and life satisfaction.

11. **Reduction in Medication Use:**

- While not a replacement for necessary medications, holistic interventions can sometimes lead to reduced reliance on certain drugs, especially in conditions like chronic pain, anxiety, or depression.

12. **Promotion of Healthy Behaviors:**

- Holistic health often involves lifestyle recommendations, promoting behaviors like healthy eating, regular exercise, and effective stress management.

In conclusion, a holistic approach provides a comprehensive model of care that recognizes the intricate interplay between various facets of an individual. By treating the whole person and not just isolated symptoms, holistic therapies offer a deeply integrative and often more sustainable pathway to health and well-being. As with any therapeutic modality, it's essential to approach holistic treatments with an evidence-based lens, ensuring interventions are backed by reputable research and adapted to each individual's unique needs.

Case Study 9

Case Study: From Fragmentation to Wholeness – Lucy's Longitudinal Journey with Holistic DBT

Background:

Name: Lucy

Age at Start of Therapy: 28

Presenting Issue: Recurrent episodes of severe depression, anxiety, emotional dysregulation, and occasional self-harm tendencies.

The Initial Approach:

Lucy's initial sessions focused on traditional DBT techniques, emphasizing cognitive-behavioral interventions, distress tolerance, and emotional regulation strategies. However, while Lucy made some progress, she frequently relapsed into old patterns.

Integrating a Holistic Approach:

Recognizing the need for a more integrative approach, Lucy's therapist, Dr. Williams, proposed blending traditional DBT with holistic elements: mindfulness practices, somatic healing techniques, and an exploration of Lucy's spiritual beliefs.

The Longitudinal Progress:

1. **Year 1:** Initial integration of daily mindfulness meditation helped Lucy develop an increased awareness of her emotional triggers. The use of journaling allowed her to recognize and track patterns.

2. **Year 2:** Lucy was introduced to somatic techniques. Yoga and tai chi classes helped her reconnect with her body, release physical tension, and enhance her emotional regulation. The introduction of breathwork exercises during heightened states of anxiety proved particularly beneficial.

3. **Year 3:** Exploration of Lucy's spiritual beliefs led her to engage in community spiritual gatherings and retreats. These provided her with a sense of belonging and purpose, substantially boosting her resilience and self-worth.

Measurable Outcomes:

1. **Psychological Assessments:** Standardized assessments showed a 60% reduction in depressive symptoms and a 50% reduction in anxiety levels by the end of Year 3.

2. **Physiological Measures:** Lucy's blood pressure and heart rate, initially on the higher side due to

chronic stress, normalized over the years, indicating improved autonomic regulation.

3. **Behavioral Changes:** Instances of self-harm became rare, with the last recorded incident being in the middle of Year 2. Lucy reported improved relationships with family and peers, attributing this to enhanced emotional regulation and effective communication techniques from DBT.

4. **Self-Reported Quality of Life:** Using a standardized quality of life scale, Lucy reported a consistent increase over the three years, noting particularly her improved sense of connection to herself and others, and a renewed sense of purpose.

Conclusion:

Lucy's journey illustrates the profound potential of a holistic DBT approach. While traditional DBT provided essential coping strategies, the integration of mindfulness, somatic healing, and spiritual exploration catered to Lucy's entire being, fostering a depth of healing not achievable by cognitive-behavioral interventions alone.

It's noteworthy to remember that holistic interventions, like all therapeutic strategies, work uniquely with each individual. Lucy's success story underscores the importance of a tailored, patient-centric approach, where therapies are adapted and integrated based on the individual's evolving needs and responses.

Reflection Space

Reflection Space: Defining Your Metrics of Success

Every therapist and client partnership has its unique rhythm, set of challenges, and benchmarks. To effectively navigate the therapeutic process, it's essential to have a clear understanding of what "success" means in your context. Reflect on the following prompts to define and refine your metrics of success:

1. **Personal Definitions:**
    - How do you currently define success in your therapeutic sessions?
    - What does a 'successful session' or 'successful therapeutic relationship' look like to you?

....
....

2. **Outcomes vs. Process:**
    - Do you measure success by the outcomes (like symptom reduction) or the process (like client engagement)?
    - Is there a balance between the two, or does one take precedence? Why?

....

....

3. **Client Feedback:**

    - How do you incorporate client feedback into your metric of success?
    - What changes or adaptations have you made based on this feedback?

....

....

4. **Holistic Milestones:**

    - With the integration of a holistic approach, what new milestones or markers of progress have you observed?
    - How do these markers differ from traditional therapy milestones?

....

....

5. **Challenges as Metrics:**

    - Can challenges or setbacks also be seen as indicators of success? If so, in what ways?

- Reflect on a time when a setback led to a significant breakthrough. What did you learn?

....
....

6. **Evolution Over Time:**

   - How have your metrics of success evolved over time?

   - Are there benchmarks that you once considered vital but no longer prioritize?

....
....

7. **Comparison with Peers:**

   - How do your metrics of success align or differ from your peers or the broader therapeutic community?

   - Are there any insights or inspirations you've drawn from others that have influenced your own metrics?

....
....

8. **Future Vision:**
    - Looking forward, how do you envision your metrics of success evolving?
    - Are there any new methods, techniques, or research findings you're excited to integrate into your measure of success?

....

....

Use this space to periodically revisit and redefine your success criteria, ensuring that they align with both your personal therapeutic philosophy and the evolving needs of your clients. It's a dynamic process, just like therapy itself. Keeping a pulse on your success metrics can help maintain a clear direction and provide a sense of fulfillment and purpose in your practice.

Chapter 9: Further Resources and Training

Books, articles, and research.

If you're looking to delve deeper into holistic healing, DBT, or any integrative approaches to therapy, here's a list of suggested readings, spanning books, articles, and research papers. While this list is not exhaustive, it provides a solid starting point for both practitioners and interested readers.

Books:

1. **DBT-Specific**

    - *Cognitive-Behavioral Treatment of Borderline Personality Disorder* by Marsha M. Linehan: The foundational text on DBT by its creator.

    - *DBT Skills Training Handouts and Worksheets* by Marsha M. Linehan: A practical guide for clinicians and clients alike.

2. **Holistic Healing**

    - *The Body Keeps the Score: Brain, Mind, and Body in the Healing of Trauma* by Bessel van der Kolk: A comprehensive look at how trauma affects the body and various holistic approaches to healing.

- *Radical Acceptance: Embracing Your Life With the Heart of a Buddha* by Tara Brach: A blending of mindfulness and compassionate practices for healing.

3. **Somatic Therapy**

    - *Waking the Tiger: Healing Trauma* by Peter A. Levine: Introduces the concept of "somatic experiencing" to heal trauma.

    - *The Revolutionary Trauma Release Process: Transcend Your Toughest Times* by David Berceli: Focuses on releasing physical tension associated with trauma.

Articles:

1. **DBT Research**

    - Neacsiu, A. D., Rizvi, S. L., & Linehan, M. M. (2010). Dialectical behavior therapy skills use as a mediator and outcome of treatment for borderline personality disorder. *Behaviour Research and Therapy, 48*(9), 832-839.

2. **Holistic Approach in Therapy**

    - Siegel, D. J. (2009). Mindful awareness, mindsight, and neural integration. *The Humanistic Psychologist, 37*(2), 137-158.

3. **Mindfulness and Mental Health**

    - Hofmann, S. G., Sawyer, A. T., Witt, A. A., & Oh, D. (2010). The effect of mindfulness-based therapy on anxiety and depression: A meta-analytic review. *Journal of consulting and clinical psychology, 78*(2), 169.

Research Papers:

1. **Effectiveness of DBT**

    - Kliem, S., Kröger, C., & Kosfelder, J. (2010). Dialectical behavior therapy for borderline personality disorder: A meta-analysis using mixed-effects modeling. *Journal of Consulting and Clinical Psychology, 78*(6), 936.

2. **Holistic Healing and Mental Health**

    - Khoury, B., Lecomte, T., Fortin, G., Masse, M., Therien, P., Bouchard, V., ... & Hofmann, S. G. (2013). Mindfulness-based therapy: A comprehensive meta-analysis. *Clinical psychology review, 33*(6), 763-771.

3. **Somatic Techniques in Psychotherapy**

    - Payne, P., Levine, P. A., & Crane-Godreau, M. A. (2015). Somatic experiencing: using interoception and proprioception as core elements of trauma therapy. *Frontiers in psychology, 6*, 93.

Remember, it's crucial to critically evaluate any source you delve into, ensuring that it aligns with current best practices, ethics, and evidence-based methodologies. As the field evolves, staying updated with the latest research and literature can be immensely beneficial for both therapists and clients.

Courses and training programs.

Engaging in continuous professional development is crucial for therapists and clinicians. If you're interested in deepening your knowledge and skills in holistic healing, DBT, and integrative therapy approaches, several training programs and courses can help. Here's a list of recommended avenues:

1. DBT-Specific Training:

- **Behavioral Tech:** Founded by Marsha M. Linehan, the creator of DBT, this organization offers a comprehensive array of DBT training, resources, and certification.
- **The Linehan Institute:** Provides trainings, certifications, and resources for DBT practitioners.

2. Mindfulness and Meditation Training:

- **Mindfulness-Based Stress Reduction (MBSR) Training:** Founded by Dr. Jon Kabat-Zinn, this program offers intensive training on mindfulness practices and their application in therapeutic contexts.

- **Insight Meditation Society (IMS):** Offers retreats and training programs focused on mindfulness and insight meditation.

3. Somatic Healing and Therapy Training:

- **The Somatic Experiencing Trauma Institute:** Offers training in Peter Levine's Somatic Experiencing method.
- **Body-Mind Centering Association:** Provides training and resources on an integrative approach to movement, touch, and voice.

4. Holistic and Integrative Therapy Approaches:

- **The Center for Integrative Therapy:** Offers training and resources for clinicians wanting to incorporate a more holistic approach into their practice.
- **Association for Comprehensive Energy Psychology (ACEP):** Provides training in energy psychology modalities, a holistic approach to psychological healing.

5. Cognitive Behavioral Therapies and Extensions:

- **The Beck Institute:** Founded by Aaron T. Beck, the father of Cognitive Therapy, this institute offers training, resources, and certifications in cognitive behavioral therapy (CBT) and its many modalities.

- **Academy of Cognitive & Behavioral Therapies:** Provides certifications, training, and conferences for professionals practicing cognitive-behavioral therapies.

6. Online Learning Platforms:

- **Coursera and Udemy:** These platforms often host courses on therapeutic techniques, mindfulness, somatic therapies, and more. Ensure courses taken here are by recognized professionals or institutions.
- **PESI:** A provider of continuing education seminars, webinars, and products for professionals. They frequently offer training in integrative and holistic therapies.

7. Conferences and Workshops:

Many professional associations, such as the American Psychological Association (APA) or the National Association of Social Workers (NASW), regularly host conferences, workshops, and seminars. They often feature sessions on new and emerging therapies.

Remember, while courses and certifications can greatly enhance your

Online resources and communities.

Online resources and communities have become invaluable for clinicians and therapists seeking to expand their knowledge, engage in discussions, and stay updated with the latest trends and research. Here's a list of online platforms, resources, and communities related to holistic healing, DBT, and integrative therapy approaches:

1. Online Resources:

- **Psychotherapy Networker:** This is an online platform that features articles, webinars, and courses for therapists on a variety of topics, including integrative approaches.
- **PsychCentral:** A longstanding resource offering articles, forums, and resources on a myriad of psychological topics.
- **The Gottman Institute Blog:** Focusing primarily on relationships, this resource is invaluable for its evidence-based strategies and insights.
- **Mindful.org:** An online hub for mindfulness practices, research, and discussions.

2. Forums & Online Communities:

- **TherapyRoute.com:** An online platform for clinicians to share knowledge, ask questions, and connect with other professionals.

- **PsychForums:** An extensive online community that covers a vast range of psychological topics. While it's not limited to professionals (clients often post here too), it provides valuable insights.
- **Reddit:** Subreddits like r/psychotherapy, r/Meditation, and r/DBTselfhelp can be places for discussion, although remember to maintain confidentiality and abide by each subreddit's rules.

3. Social Media Groups:

- **Facebook:** There are many private groups dedicated to therapists, where members discuss therapy modalities, share resources, and seek advice. Examples include "Dialectical Behaviour Therapy" and "Mindfulness and Psychotherapy."
- **LinkedIn Groups:** There are numerous therapy-focused groups on LinkedIn that foster networking, sharing of articles, and discussions on the latest trends in therapy.

4. Webinars & Video Platforms:

- **SimplePractice Learning:** This platform offers numerous CE-approved webinars on various topics related to therapy.
- **YouTube:** Many professionals and institutions have channels dedicated to therapy techniques, discussions, and seminars. Ensure you follow

channels that are evidence-based and adhere to professional standards.

5. Research Platforms & Journals:

- **Google Scholar:** A freely accessible web search engine that indexes scholarly articles across an array of publishing formats and disciplines.

- **ResearchGate:** Allows researchers to share their papers, and you can often find the latest research here.

6. Blogs & Podcasts:

- **The Trauma Therapist Podcast:** Covers a range of topics related to trauma therapy, including holistic approaches.

- **The Science of Psychotherapy:** A podcast that dives into the science and art of psychotherapy.

7. Online Directories:

- **GoodTherapy.org:** Aside from being a directory for therapists, it also has an extensive blog and resource section, including topics on integrative therapies.

- **Psychology Today:** Known for its therapist directory, it also boasts a plethora of articles written by professionals on a myriad of topics.

When engaging in online communities, always be cautious about maintaining the confidentiality of your clients and seeking supervision for specific clinical questions. Furthermore, always ensure that the information you obtain online is credible and evidence-based.

References

1. **Linehan, M. M. (2014).** *DBT® Skills Training Manual*. Guilford Press.

2. **Kabat-Zinn, J. (2013).** *Full catastrophe living: Using the wisdom of your body and mind to face stress, pain, and illness*. Bantam.

3. **Levine, P. A. (2010).** *In an unspoken voice: How the body releases trauma and restores goodness*. North Atlantic Books.

4. **Van der Kolk, B. (2014).** *The body keeps the score: Brain, mind, and body in the healing of trauma*. Viking.

5. **Siegel, D. J. (2010).** *The mindful therapist: A clinician's guide to mindsight and neural integration*. W. W. Norton & Company.

6. **Ogden, P., & Fisher, J. (2015).** *Sensorimotor psychotherapy: Interventions for trauma and attachment*. W. W. Norton & Company.

7. **Beck, A. T., Davis, D. D., & Freeman, A. (2015).** *Cognitive therapy of personality disorders*. Guilford publications.

8. **Chodron, P. (2000).** *When things fall apart: Heart advice for difficult times*. Shambhala Publications.

9. **Hanson, R. (2009).** *Buddha's brain: The practical neuroscience of happiness, love & wisdom*. New Harbinger Publications.

10. **Germer, C. K., & Neff, K. D. (2013).** *Self-compassion in clinical practice*. Journal of Clinical Psychology, 69(8), 856-867.

11. **Siegel, R. D. (2010).** *The mindfulness solution: Everyday practices for everyday problems*. Guilford Press.

12. **Follette, V. M., & Pistorello, J. (2007).** *Finding life beyond trauma: Using acceptance and commitment therapy to heal from post-traumatic stress and trauma-related problems*. New Harbinger Publications.

13. **Payne, P., Crane-Godreau, M. A., & Lutz, A. (2015).** *Meditative movement for depression and anxiety*. Frontiers in Psychiatry, 6, 94.

14. **Oschman, J. L., Chevalier, G., & Brown, R. (2015).** *The effects of grounding (earthing) on inflammation, the immune response, wound healing, and prevention and treatment of chronic inflammatory and autoimmune diseases*. Journal of Inflammation Research, 8, 83.

15. **Rothschild, B. (2000).** *The body remembers: The psychophysiology of trauma and trauma treatment*. W. W. Norton & Company.

16. **Gilbert, P. (2010).** *Compassion focused therapy: Distinctive features*. Routledge.